H A M L Y N
C R E A T I V E   C R A F T S

PATCHWORK &
QUILTING

HAMLYN
CREATIVE CRAFTS

PATCHWORK & QUILTING

Brigitte Staub-Wachsmuth

HAMLYN

Dedication:
To Dr Nikki and Grady Bennett
of Orlando, Florida, for all their
encouragement and assistance.

Contents

Patchwork Sampler
(1982, Brigitte Staub-Wachsmuth)
Size: 205 × 240 cm/80¾ × 94½ in
Each block of this quilt is a different design. All are traditional American motifs.

Foreword

In January 1982 my husband's work took us to Orlando, Florida. I heartily welcomed the move in the hope that I would at last be able to buy an American patchwork quilt, preferably an antique one. I had heard about them from a neighbour who had a quilt from America decorating her bedroom wall. My greatest wish was to own a quilt like hers. If I couldn't make my own I would buy one, whatever the cost!

It was to be almost two months before I found my first authentic quilt, but it proved to be so expensive and such a glaring yellow that I could not bring myself to buy it.

I involved my husband, too, in my hunt for quilts and one evening he came across a newspaper advertisement for a course in quilting. 'If you must buy a quilt,' he said, 'you should at least get to know something about them first.'

This was said half-jokingly but I took him seriously and actually enrolled for a quilting course for beginners at Valencia Community College.

Highly sceptical, and thinking that I would learn next to nothing about patchwork and quilts, I started Dr Nikki Bennett's class. After a short introduction she promised us that we would all have made a quilt by the end of the nine-week course. I looked at her in amazement. Could I possibly make a whole quilt in such a short time?

Dr Bennett was adamant: 'Yes, you'll do it, even without a sewing machine! But you'll have to do some work on it at home of course!'

And she was right! By using up-to-date methods of American patchwork, at the end of the course I was able to take home with me not only a finished, hand-sewn quilt top (see illustration page 6) but also a finished quilted cushion and a wall quilt.

From then on our lives were transformed. It is now taken for granted that my quilt frame is set up in the living room while the kitchen doubles as a cutting room. We never miss a quilt exhibition and ideas for future quilts are put forward and discussed by every member of the family.

The interplay of colours, the variety of designs and the creative possibilities of this hobby, make it as fascinating to me today as it was in the beginning. After that first course, I took two further courses in patchwork and joined the Cabin Fever Quilters of Orlando, Florida, and the National Quilters. Both are organisations that hold monthly meetings for men and women where they can talk about the market for quilts, pass on specific techniques and show off their finished products.

Now I would like to share my passion with others and to show them a method of patchwork which will enable them to make a quilt relatively quickly and encourage them to try their hand at different designs.

In my experience the best way to learn as much as possible, as quickly as possible about patchwork and quilting is to have a go at making a sampler quilt. This is a quilt that brings together numerous examples of the various patchwork and quilting methods.

Sampler quilts were often made in the past – one example is a friendship quilt. These are authentic quilts in themselves which can be extremely artistic.

Each of the blocks that make up the quilt is different and forms a specific pattern. (In patchwork the word 'pattern' refers to the design made by arranging pieces of fabric to form a block of the quilt.) Although these patterns are sewn together or appliquéd in different ways, you always end up with the same sized *blocks*, each $12\frac{1}{2}$ in (31.8cm) square. (In this book I have purposely stuck to the original size of American patchwork blocks. All patterns from America are in this size and so you will easily be able to combine them with the patterns given in this book.)

Finally, a word about the plan of the book. The chapters are arranged in order of difficulty so it is a good idea, especially for beginners, to work through systematically. I wish you enjoyment and success in your work.

Even quilts have a history

What is a quilt?

The word 'quilt' is English in origin and refers to a padded bed covering, although such a definition can hardly describe some of the masterpieces which went under this name in the days when America was a colony or those which are still being made today in America and Europe.

A quilt always consists of three layers:

- The quilt cover, known as the quilt top, is made either by joining small scraps of fabric to form a pattern or richly decorated with appliqué.
- The middle layer used to be made from cotton or wool wadding, but is now usually made of polyester.
- The underside of the quilt is usually made from one single length of fabric, often the same fabric used for the border of the quilt top.

These three layers are sewn together by a method known as 'quilting'.

There are three different types of quilt:

1. Patchwork quilts which have a quilt top made by sewing together many separate pieces of fabric.
2. Appliquéd quilts which have a quilt top usually made out of one continuous piece of fabric onto which artistic designs are appliquéd.
3. Quilts which have the top made in a plain or patterned fabric are called wholecloth quilts. The decorative effect of these quilts is entirely the result of the intricacy of the quilting.

A detail from the Album Quilt on the opposite page. The fruit basket is part appliquéd, part embroidered.

We learned it from the Chinese

It was apparently the Chinese who invented the idea of making winter clothes from three layers of fabric. The warming middle-layer was held firmly in place by quilt-stitching. This technique then spread from China throughout the Orient.

In the Middle Ages knights wore quilted undershirts to make their heavy armour more comfortable. When they came back from the Crusades it was not long before the women at home recognised the advantages of quilted bedcovers and clothing. The idea caught on in England especially, where in the 14th century the weather was unusually cold.

Numerous quilts were made at this time by rich and poor alike. At first they were plain and purely functional but it was not long before decorative and ornamental quilting techniques were developed. Portuguese merchants brought

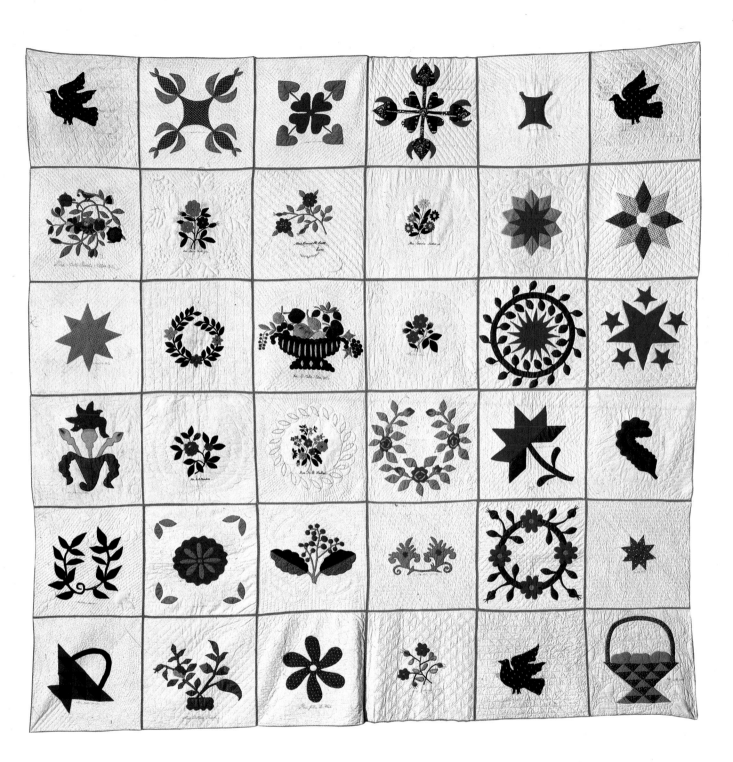

Album Quilt

Size: 220 × 220 cm/86½ × 86½ in, made in 1870 in Vermont, USA
Cotton and wool are the materials that make up this sampler quilt. Each of the 36
blocks of pattern is appliquéd and some also have embroidery. Each of the squares was
made by a different person and is signed with the maker's name. Album or friendship
quilts like this one were often made by a girl's friends as a gift, possibly for a birthday.
(Source: Badisches Landesmuseum, Karlsruhe)

Oriental quilts to Europe and their intricate designs were widely copied. So quilts gradually developed from functional household articles into expensive, richly decorated works of art.

In the 15th century, the Trapunto technique was developed in Italy. Here the quilting design was made on a white background, with individual decorative elements given extra padding to make them stand out and give them solidity. At the same time the French were making quilts from silk and damask, while in Spain brocade and velvet were being used.

The origins of the American quilt

Quilts already had a long European history behind them when in 1620 they travelled to the New World in the baggage of the Pilgrim Fathers. On board ship they proved indispensable, being used both as bedding and as room dividers, for *The Mayflower* was not a ship providing the comfort of cabins.

When the Pilgrim Fathers were eventually able to land (near what is today Plymouth, Massachusetts) in the spring of 1621, most had been forced to spend the winter on board ship since there was no shelter on land from the bitter cold. As a result, many of the quilts had become badly worn. Since ships from England were extremely infrequent there was little opportunity to buy new fabrics, so the old quilts had to be patched. For this the women used anything handy: pieces of old dresses and suits that still had some wear in them or anything else that seemed suitable. The first patchwork quilts were thus made from necessity and were anything but artistic.

Obtaining cloth remained a problem even when the lives of the immigrants became more normal.

Star Patchwork
Size: 190 × 194 cm/74¾ × 76¼ in, made at the end of the 19th century in Ontario, Canada. The star is made from many small diamonds, the flower motifs are appliquéd. (Source: Municipal Museum, Alzey)

For as England, fearful of losing its monopoly, would not allow looms or other tools of the clothing industry to be exported to the New World, no local cloth was available and women had to rely on the infrequent and expensive shipments from the mother country. Thus quilts continued to be made from left-over material and patches. But now the quiltmakers began to make a virtue of necessity. They began to invent patterns and took pride in creating complicated and interesting patchwork designs. So it was that patchwork as we know it today was an invention of the New World, and modern Americans are still extremely proud of this craft.

Over the years patchwork and quilting came to have a social significance for the people of America, country of wide open spaces. During the long winters the women sat at home piecing together their quilt tops. Once spring began and it was again possible to go out, they invited each other to quilting bees.

As many neighbours were invited as there were seats around the quilting frame and together they completed one quilt after another. It gave them a chance to catch up on news. The lady of the house provided meals and towards evening husbands or boyfriends would join them. They ate and drank together and often the evening ended with dancing.

As well as making up their own

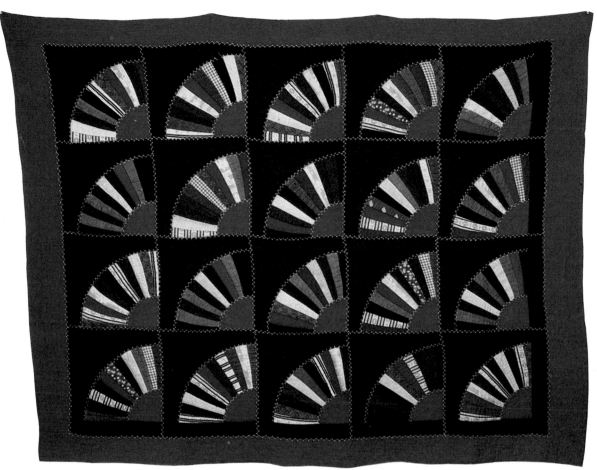

Grandmother's Fan Patchwork
Size: 155 × 200 cm/61 × 78¾ in, made towards the end of the 19th century in Ontario, Canada.
An unusual feature of this patchwork is the joining of the individual patches by visible zig-zag stitching.
(Source: Municipal Museum, Alzey)

quilts these groups of women sometimes met to make a quilt for a special occasion. For instance, every young man received a 'freedom quilt' on his twentieth birthday. This would be made by his mother, sisters and female friends out of their prettiest clothes. It symbolised the young man's independence now that he no longer had to rely on his mother and sisters for his quilt. These quilts often accompanied the young men on journeys of adventure, and due to all the wear and tear that this entailed very few have survived.

Other kinds of friendship quilts were also made. Usually a girl's mother arranged a friendship quilt party as a surprise for a birthday,

engagement or wedding. The guests arrived early in the morning, each bringing her own materials. They then agreed on which pattern blocks to use and often competed for the chance to make the most difficult or complicated elements. The individual blocks were then signed with the name of the maker and given to the girl.

Friendship quilts like these are very popular even today. In almost every quilt club it is usual to make and exchange friendship blocks.

For a memorial quilt the clothes of someone who had died were made into a quilt. These were usually sombre in colour and all the deceased person's friends, both male and female, worked on the quilt as a

token of respect.

Before a girl could marry she had to make thirteen quilts. The thirteenth quilt was not made until the girl became engaged and it became her bride or marriage quilt. However, in many areas it was the custom for the bride's girlfriends to make a bride quilt for it was thought unlucky for her to make her own. Heart motifs were the most popular designs for a bride quilt. If you come across an antique quilt with heart motifs you can be sure it was once a bridal quilt.

All quilts made before 1750 were entirely of patchwork. From 1750 to around 1850 appliquéd quilts became popular. Flower designs – usually spread over the entire quilt –

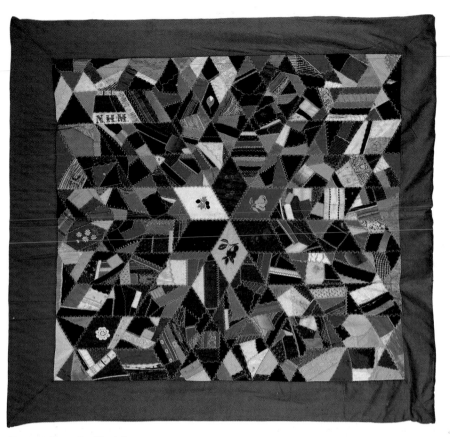

were thought particularly elegant and were highly prized.

From 1850 onwards the actual quilting became more important. Quilts were made in white cotton with a design of quilting stitches. These were known as white work. At this time it was usual to turn patchwork quilts over to display only the lines of quilting on the back. Even today quiltmakers will show you the reverse of their quilts and pay as much attention to this as to the top.

Interestingly, many more antique appliqué quilts have survived than patchwork ones. This is because at the time they were made appliqué quilts were more highly valued and were kept for special occasions. Patchwork quilts, on the other hand, were for everyday use and so wore out more quickly.

In the 1970s, patchwork and quilting underwent something of a renaissance in America. Once more

Crazy Star Quilt (above)
Size: 160 × 170 cm/63 × 67 in, made around 1890 in Vermont, USA
This luxurious quilt was made in silk and satin. The central star is surrounded by a crazy-quilt pattern. (Source: Max Berk Textile Museum, Heidelberg-Ziegelhausen)

Rosettes (right)
Size 86 × 96 cm/33¾ × 37¾ in, made around 1870 in Co. Durham, England Artistic patchwork was also produced in the Old World, as can be seen from this Rosette patchwork made in silk and rep. (Source: Max Berk Textile Museum, Heidelberg-Ziegelhausen)

quiltmaking has become a popular pastime. In every large town you will find a quilt shop selling the necessary fabrics and materials.

The modern quiltmaker uses cottons specially made for quilt-making; there are a multitude of books and magazines devoted to patchwork and quilting. It is once more fashionable to belong to a quilt club and to be able to talk about quilts at dinner parties.

Often in quiltmaking, the pattern blocks and quilting designs have been passed down from one generation to the next, so that many of the quilts being made in the United States today give a good idea of what the original quilts must have looked like. Names of patterns still in use – some of which are included in this book – have also been handed down and provide an image of the world of the past. Some of the names are inspired by aspects of daily life, such as the Sawtooth pattern or the Basket of Scraps. Many appliqué patterns have names from the plant or animal kingdoms, such as Wild Rose or Honey Bee. Another popular source of names was the area where the pattern originated: Ohio Star or Texas Star. Names taken from Bible stories were popular too, like Jacob's Ladder.

Even today most quiltmakers give a name either to the pattern blocks or to the whole quilt – either using the traditional name of the pattern or inventing new names of their own.

A quilt is much more than an item of padded clothing or a bed-cover. It is a work of art and quiltmakers are justly proud of their skill and creativity. This pride is shown in the fact that their quilts are given names. Most quilts are also signed and dated. You will find, once you have finished your first quilt, that you too will become captivated by the creative possibilities of the technique, so that I am sure your first quilt will by no means be your last.

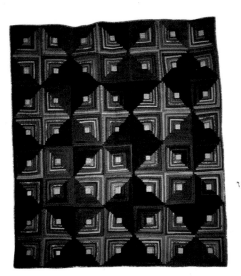

Bear's Paws (above)
*Size 168 × 205 cm/66¼ × 80¾ in, made around 1910 in Ohio, USA
This quilt is typical Amish work, a sect with a strict traditional way of life. They still use a limited number of patterns and plain materials for quiltmaking today.*

Mennonite Log Cabin (left)
*Size: 170 × 198 cm/67 × 78 in, made around 1880 in Ontario, Canada
(Both photos: Max Berk Textile Museum, Heidelberg-Ziegelhausen)*

Short guide to materials

Before starting on your first quilt you will need to buy or find the following materials:

To make the templates:
Cardboard (2 mm/¹⁄₁₀ in thick), tracing paper, drawing paper, paper scissors or card knife, glue, pencil, ruler.

To sew the patchwork:
Five or six different cotton fabrics in toning shades, dressmaking scissors, washable textile marker or dressmaker's chalk, pins, needles, tacking thread, sewing machine (if available), neutral-coloured sewing thread.

To prepare the patchwork for quilting:
Polyester wadding (available in 90 and 140 cm/35½ and 55 in widths), buy enough to go the whole length of the quilt for the lining. (If your quilt is wider than 140 cm/55 in, you will need twice the length.)
  Plain or patterned fabric for the reverse of the quilt, twice the length of the quilt-top plus 30 cm/11¾ in seam allowance for the edges.

For quilting:
Quilting needles, quilting thread (strong cotton-covered polyester thread), quilting frame (if available).

Choice of fabric and colours

Cotton fabrics are ideal for the beginner. They do not slip and they retain their crease, even when made just with the fingers. And when you come to quilting, cotton is again easy to use. Other fabrics can of course be used but as they are more difficult to work with I will not be dealing with them in this introductory book. When choosing colours always bear in mind where you plan to use the finished quilt and choose colours to go with their surroundings. For a sampler quilt you will need five or six different fabrics of different designs. You should always include a plain coloured fabric on which you can appliqué and choose the remaining five or six patterned fabrics to tone with this base colour.

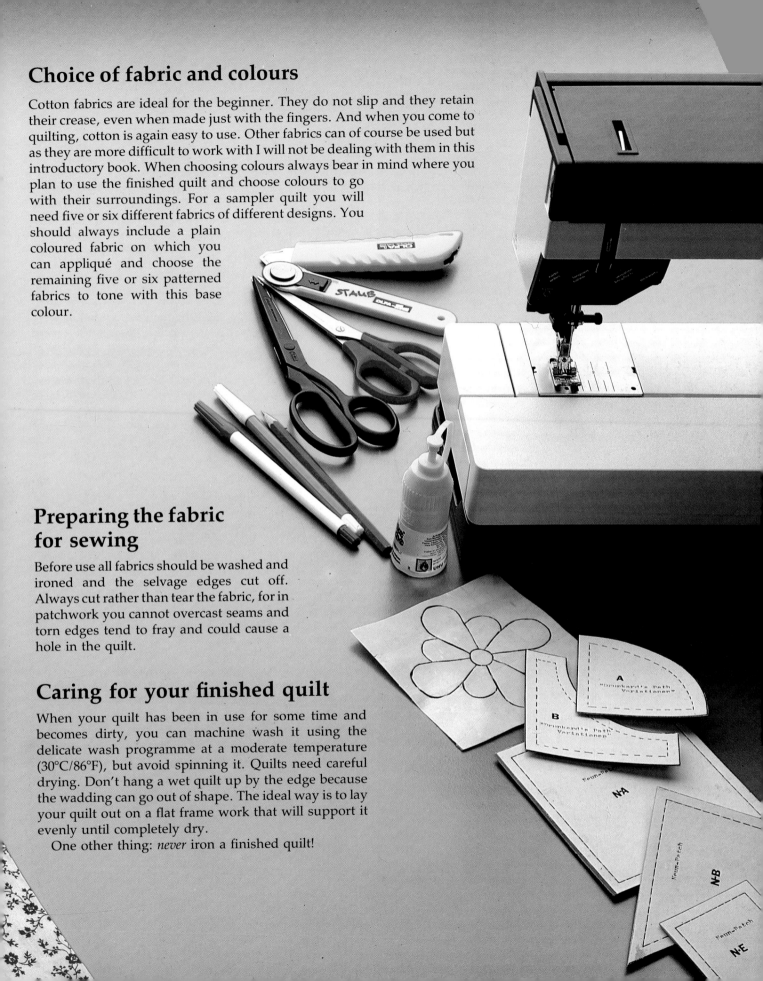

Preparing the fabric for sewing

Before use all fabrics should be washed and ironed and the selvage edges cut off. Always cut rather than tear the fabric, for in patchwork you cannot overcast seams and torn edges tend to fray and could cause a hole in the quilt.

Caring for your finished quilt

When your quilt has been in use for some time and becomes dirty, you can machine wash it using the delicate wash programme at a moderate temperature (30°C/86°F), but avoid spinning it. Quilts need careful drying. Don't hang a wet quilt up by the edge because the wadding can go out of shape. The ideal way is to lay your quilt out on a flat frame work that will support it evenly until completely dry.

One other thing: *never* iron a finished quilt!

Making a pattern block

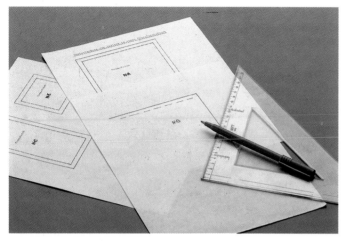

Making the templates

To enable the separate parts of the pattern block to be cut exactly to size work from templates. This is extremely important, for if the sections do not fit exactly it will be impossible to sew the patchwork block together correctly when that stage is reached. In this example Jacob's Ladder pattern is demonstrated which consists of a nine-patch block. You will find full-size template patterns for nine-patch blocks on page 30. For Jacob's Ladder we need templates B and E. Using tracing paper*, you can trace these from the book (*see the short guide to materials on page 14). Make sure you trace very carefully so that all the sections will fit together exactly.

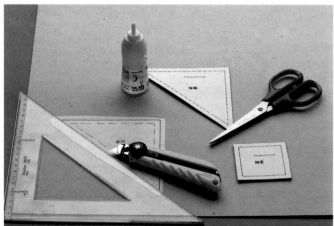

Roughly cut out the triangle (B) and the square (E) from the tracing paper and glue onto 2 mm/$\frac{1}{10}$ in cardboard. Then cut the templates from the cardboard. It is again important to work extremely accurately! You will get really clean edges if you use a Stanley knife or craft knife. When you come to cut, it is a good idea to glue a small piece of fine sandpaper onto the back of the templates to hold them firmly on the fabric.

Make all the templates you need for a particular pattern block at the same time and mark each one clearly to avoid getting them mixed up.

Cutting the fabric

For each of the pattern blocks described in the following chapters you will be told how many different fabrics you need. (In our example, Jacob's Ladder we need four different fabrics.) First, place the cardboard template on the wrong side of the fabric and then draw round the edge with an impermanent marker. The template includes all seam allowances so that you do not have to waste fabric by leaving spaces between the pieces.
(For our example we need: Fabric 1: 4 of B, fabric 2: 4 of B, fabric 3: 10 of E, fabric 4: 10 of E.)

If you are going to sew the sections together by hand you should mark in the seam line 6 mm/$\frac{1}{4}$ in from the edge of the material before you begin cutting out.

Sewing the patches together

Once you have cut out all the sections, spread them out in front of you to make the pattern block. It is a good idea to lay them out in the small squares that make up the pattern block, as in the picture. The number of squares depends on the basic block group to which the pattern belongs. In our example we have chosen a pattern from the nine-patch blocks and so we have nine small squares.

It is very important to sort the pieces in this way before you start. For when you sew together a patchwork block you always build it up gradually from small beginnings, and by laying it out in this way it becomes clear which sections have to be sewn together first.

In a nine-patch pattern, the first thing you have to do is to make the nine patches. The best order in which to proceed is shown in the drawing. First parts 1 and 2, then parts 3 and 4 and then parts 5 and 6 are joined. Do not begin any actual sewing until you are certain about the order in which you are to do it.

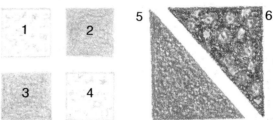

For machine sewing always place the pieces right-sides together and, with the edge of the foot following the cut edge exactly, you will automatically sew along the right seam line. (In European machines the distance between the sewing needle and the edge of the foot is 6 mm = $\frac{1}{4}$ in.)

When you have sewn two sections together, pull out a little thread from the machine and sew the next two sections together without cutting the thread. In the end all the pieces will hang together in one long line and can be easily separated.

If you have not got a sewing machine, or if you prefer sewing by hand, proceed exactly as described above. The sections are again placed right-sides together and sewn along the line you have marked. Always use four running stitches followed by one backstitch. At the end of the seam fasten off the thread with a few backstitches.

Again when sewing by hand you should assemble the nine small patches first before joining them to make the pattern block.

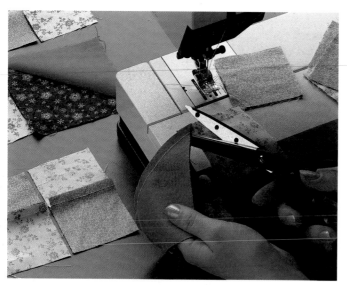

Do not cut the threads to separate individual patches until you have completed all the seams that can be done in the first stage. (This only applies to machine sewing of course, for when sewing by hand the patches are assembled separately.)

Next, fold all the seams to one side and press them down by hand. In patchwork – unlike normal dressmaking – seams should *never* be ironed open. This applies to all seams, not just those within the pattern block! It is unnecessary to overcast seams, as the zig-zag stitch tends to distort them.

In the next stage, you continue assembling the patches following the pattern you have chosen. It is best to work with a picture of the pattern in front of you so that you can keep checking which pieces fit where. Whenever two seams meet, place the fabric together with the seams lying in opposite directions. Then pin together exactly where the seams meet. Always place the pins at right angles to the line to be sewn so that you can machine over them easily. Do not remove the pins until the whole seam is complete.

Now continue sewing the sections together as described above, leaving a continuous thread between them (when machine sewing). Always keep in mind what the final pattern looks like. After each stage, lay out the pieces in their assigned places so that it is always clear which pieces should be sewn together and in what order. It is very annoying to find that you have sewn the wrong sections together and extremely difficult to rectify the mistake. Since the edges have not been overcast they fray easily when you try to separate them, making the piece of fabric useless.

When the nine patches (or the number required for the particular pattern block you are making) are complete, lay them out and check that they actually make the desired pattern. If you have made a mistake it is not too difficult to put it right at this stage: you will simply have to recut and resew the patch in question. If everything is all right you can begin sewing the block together.

The block consists of three rows (or two in the case of the four-patch block) which should be sewn together as shown in the drawing. Once again the assembled patches are placed right-sides together so that the seam is visible on the wrong side. Use plenty of pins when preparing this stage, especially at the tricky spots where two or more seams meet. Here again you should place the pins at right angles to the seam you are going to sew so that you can sew over them easily. If you are doubtful about only pinning the sections together before sewing them, you can of course carefully tack the sections in place and remove the tacks later.

Below: *Only when the whole block has been sewn together should it be ironed. (When you are actually sewing, it is enough to flatten and turn the seams by hand which presents no problems if you are sewing on cotton.) When ironing, fold all the seams in the same direction. A patchwork block should be ironed on the wrong side first and then on the right side.*

Right: *This is what the completed Jacob's Ladder pattern block should look like. The untrimmed edges will later disappear under the border.*

Assembling the quilt top

The number of pattern blocks you will have to make depends on the size of the finished quilt. Only when all the patchwork blocks are complete should you begin assembling the individual blocks to make the quilt-top. For a first sampler quilt like ours, you will need 12 pattern blocks for a single quilt around 200 cm/78¾ in long. If for any reason you need the quilt to be longer, you can make the borders wider and plan in advance an extra row of blocks. For a double quilt you will need 20 pattern blocks (five widthways and four lengthways).

Before you sew the lattice strips to the blocks you will have to decide on the most attractive way of arranging the blocks. To do this, lay the blocks out on a light-coloured cloth and keep arranging and rearranging them until you feel you have the best possible arrangement. Next you should number the blocks and mark them with a scrap of paper.

Now you have to work out how much material you will need for the borders. Our sample quilt is to be around 200 cm/78¾ in in length. Border A (also called frame A) should be 6 cm/2⅓ in wide, border B 10 cm/4 in and border C 14 cm/5½ in. (The dotted lines show where the various parts of the border should be joined.) Borders A and C should be in the same fabric, border B in one of the patterned fabrics used in the blocks. Next, using a schematic drawing like the one given here, work out how much material you will need for *each* border. Bear in mind that you will need an extra 6 mm/¼ in seam allowance top and bottom and each side. To make cutting the borders easier I usually make cardboard templates to the required size (plus 6 mm/¼ in seam allowance on each side).

The best way to cut the borders is with a roller cutter. Note that here once again, as elsewhere in patchwork, the fabric should not be torn or it will fray.

In my experience it is always a good idea at this stage of the work to make a schematic drawing on which you can mark vital information such as the length and width of the borders and the order of the pattern blocks. With this drawing in front of you, the abstract reckoning up of

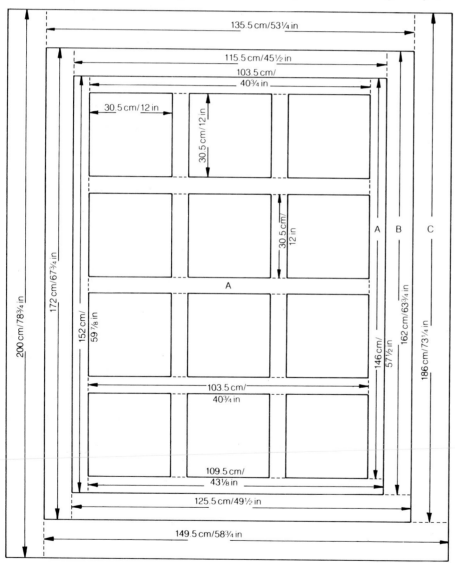

Schematic drawing to help you work out fabric quantities for the borders and lattice

Sampler Quilt *(1983, Felisa Erb-Mena)*
Size: 165 × 205 cm/65 × 80¾ in
In this typical sampler quilt all twelve blocks have different patchwork patterns
although the same fabrics have been used in each. The lattice and borders give the
blocks unity.

fabric quantities becomes much easier.

You have already decided on the best arrangement of the blocks for the quilt-top. To avoid mixing them up when you come to assemble them it is a good idea to attach a small label to each block identifying its position. For this you can either use the system of figures and letters shown in the diagram below or any other system of your own. The main thing is that it must make clear where the block will eventually go in the quilt. I usually leave the labels in place until all the lattice strips have been attached to the blocks.

For a sampler quilt you should always include borders. They serve firstly to separate the different motifs from one another and secondly, being of uniform colour, help to make them into a unified whole. If, however, you prefer to make a quilt without borders, in which the pattern blocks are sewn directly onto one another, and there is no reason why you shouldn't do so, the principle is exactly the same. First, by moving the blocks around, you can establish the best arrangement of the blocks with one another and as a whole. Next, mark each block with its position. Then the blocks can be sewn directly together. First they are sewn together to make rows. Then the first and second rows are sewn together the third row added to these, and so on.

Joining in the lattice strips

The diagram alongside sets out the order in which the lattice strips should be sewn to the blocks.

First strip A is sewn to block 1a. Then block 1b is attached, followed by another strip A. Continue in this way until all the rows are completed. The completed row is then sewn to lattice strip B, then the second row is attached, and so on until all the rows have been joined together.

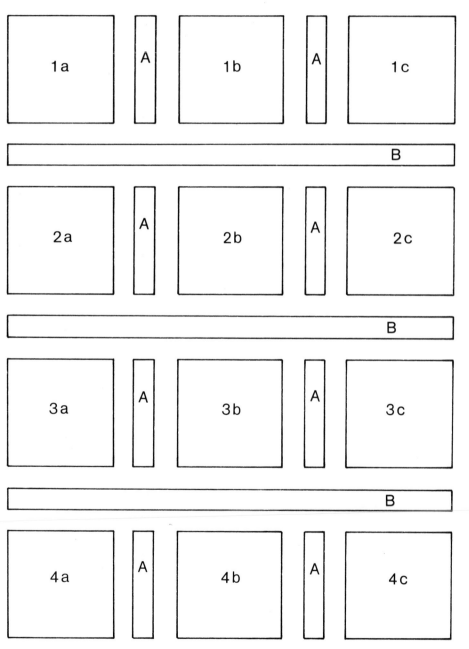

Joining in the lattice strips

Adding the borders

It only remains now to attach the outer borders to the centre panel and the quilt-top is complete. The diagram below shows the order in which the borders are worked. You should always work from the middle outwards. The first border, A, should be in the same fabric and of the same width as the lattice strips. The second border should be 10 cm/ 4 in wide and can be of a patterned fabric, preferably one of the main ones used in the pattern blocks, or one that contains all the colours used for your quilt. The third border, 14 cm/5½ in wide, should be in the same fabric as border A and form a frame to the whole quilt top. Eventually there will be a fourth border (not shown here) formed by turning the fabric used for the backing of the quilt over the edges of the quilt-top. This makes border C look rather smaller. If you want to avoid this you can either use the same fabric for the back of the quilt as for border C or finish off the edges of the quilt with bias binding.

To finish off, the completed quilt-top should be ironed once more, making sure that all seams are pressed over to one side and not ironed out open.

Now is the time to embroider your name and the date the quilt was made on a convenient corner, or to mark the quilt up for quilting.

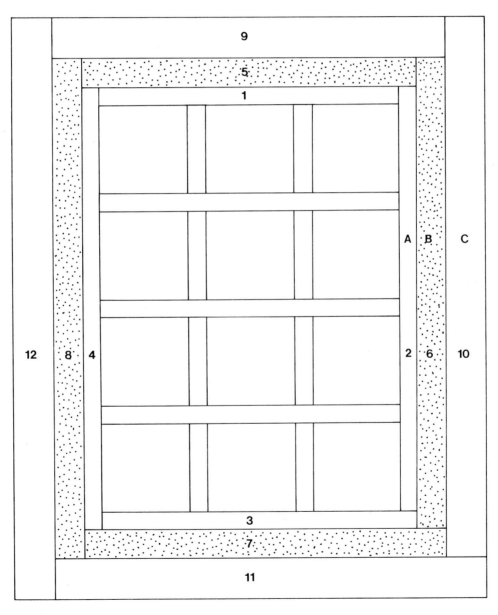

When attaching the borders always work from the middle outwards.

The nine-patch block

All the patterns included in this section are based on a square subdivided into nine equal parts (patches). The dimensions of *the basic square* are the traditional dimensions of American patchwork – 12 × 12 in (or 30.5 × 30.5 cm). Each patch can then be subdivided again into triangles or squares (see diagram 2).

(Template patterns in the actual size, which you can use to make your own templates, can be found on page 30 at the end of this section.)

The patterns are made up by arranging these templates in different ways. All the pattern blocks included in this and the following sections are traditional American patterns as used by pioneer women.

The choice of colours and fabrics is entirely up to you. The examples given are intended only as a guide. Remember when you come to sew together the nine-patch blocks that in each case they consist basically of nine equal squares. You should begin by assembling each of the nine patches and then join them to make the complete pattern block.

The Jacob's Ladder shown in the 'Making a pattern block' section (page 16) is also a nine-patch block and you can find templates for this one on page 30 too.

In the following pages the nine-patch patterns are given in each case in the form of a photograph, a diagram and a short working guide.

The photo shows what the finished block looks like. The diagram alongside contains the following information:
1. Letters indicating which templates you need and how many of each.
2. The different colour tones in each diagram show the arrangement of the different fabrics. Each fabric has its own colour tone.
3. The broken lines in the diagram show the quilting lines recommended for the pattern in question.

The quilting is not done until the whole quilt-top is completed, so you need not worry about these lines for the time being. Details of quilting are given on page 58.

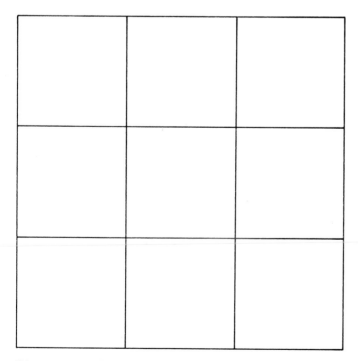

Diagram 1: *Schematic diagram of the division of the basic square into nine patches.*

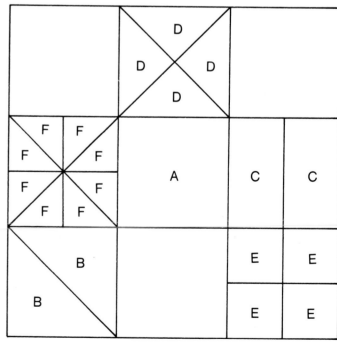

Diagram 2: *The individual patches can be further subdivided into smaller triangles and squares.*

Nine-Patch Sampler *(1985, Brigitte Staub-Wachsmuth)*
Size: 170 × 210 cm/67 × 82½ in
All the blocks in this quilt are nine-patch blocks. They show the great variety
of patterns which can be achieved with the nine-patch templates.

Traditional nine-patch block patterns

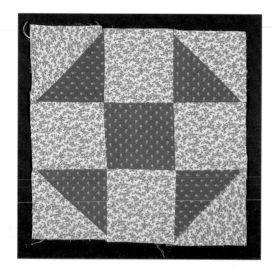

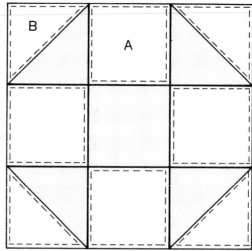

Shoofly
Materials:
2 different fabrics
Templates A, B
(page 30)
Cutting:
Fabric 1: 4 of A
*   4 of B*
Fabric 2: 1 of A
*   4 of B*

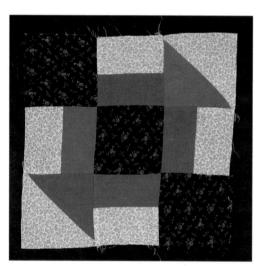

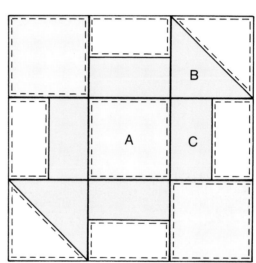

Nine-Patch-Variation
Materials:
3 different fabrics
Templates A, B, C
(page 30)
Cutting:
Fabric 1: 3 of A
Fabric 2: 2 of B
*   4 of C*
Fabric 3: 2 of B
*   4 of C*

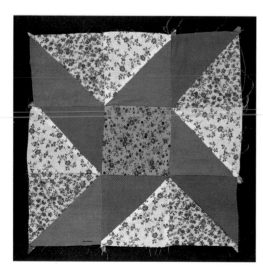

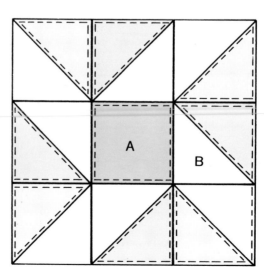

Box-Quilt
Materials:
4 different fabrics
Templates A, B
(page 30)
Cutting:
Fabric 1: 1 of A
Fabric 2: 8 of B
Fabric 3: 4 of B
Fabric 4: 4 of B

Ohio Star
Materials:
3 different fabrics
Templates A, D
(page 30)
Cutting:
Fabric 1: 4 of A
*   4 of D*
Fabric 2: 1 of A
*   8 of D*
Fabric 3: 4 of D

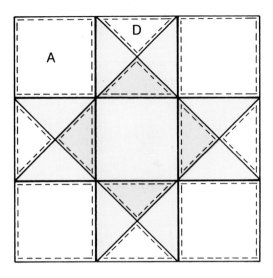

Card Trick
Materials:
5 different fabrics
Templates B, D
(page 30)
Cutting:
Fabric 1: 4 of B
*   4 of D*
Fabric 2: 2 of B
*   2 of D*
Fabric 3: 2 of B
*   2 of D*
Fabric 4: 2 of B
*   2 of D*
Fabric 5: 2 of B
*   2 of D*

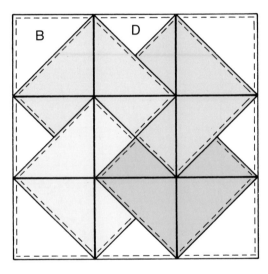
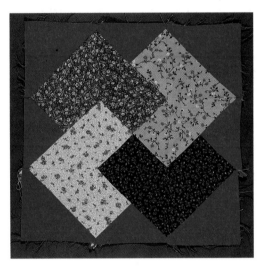

Album Nine Patches
Materials:
3 different fabrics
Templates A, B, E, F
(page 30)
Cutting:
Fabric 1: 1 of A
*   8 of F*
Fabric 2: 4 of A
Fabric 3: 4 of B
*   4 of E*

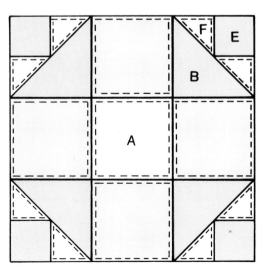

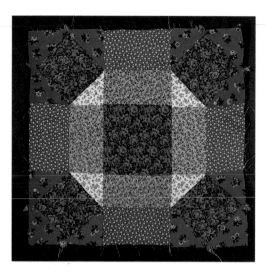

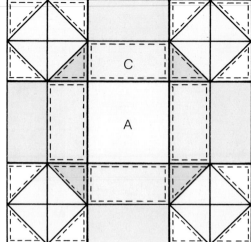

Rolling Stone

Materials:
5 different fabrics
Templates A, C, F
(page 30)
Cutting:
Fabric 1: 1 of A
*   16 of F*
Fabric 2: 4 of C
Fabric 3: 4 of C
Fabric 4: 12 of F
Fabric 5: 4 of F

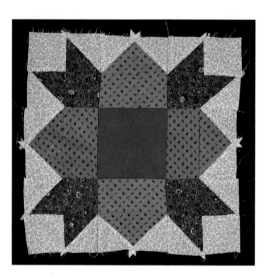

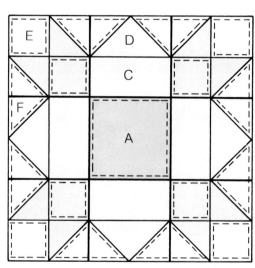

Weather Vane

Materials:
4 different fabrics
Templates A, C, D, E, F
(page 30)
Cutting:
Fabric 1: 1 of A
Fabric 2: 4 of C
*   4 of D*
Fabric 3: 4 of E
*   8 of F*
Fabric 4: 4 of E
*   16 of F*

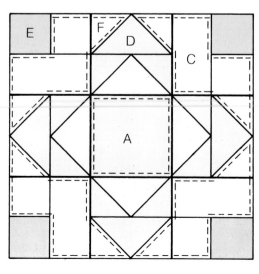

Aunt Suckey's Choice

Materials:
4 different fabrics
Templates A, C, D, E, F
(page 30)
Cutting:
Fabric 1: 1 of A
*   4 of D*
*   8 of F*
Fabric 2: 4 of D
Fabric 3: 4 of C
*   4 of E*
*   8 of F*
Fabric 4: 4 of E

Sunshine and Shadow (1984, Brigitte Staub-Wachsmuth)

Size: 130 × 130 cm/51 × 51 in

This distinctive pattern is made by arranging squares of different colours side by side. You can work from template A from the nine-patch block. It is a good idea to make a preliminary sketch to use as a guide when sewing your squares together. The squares should be joined to make horizontal rows and then the rows sewn together working from top to bottom. When deciding on the colour composition you should imagine that you are standing in the sun, looking into the shadow. The overall design of the Sunshine and Shadow pattern works best with colours ranging from light to dark.

29

Template patterns for nine-patch blocks

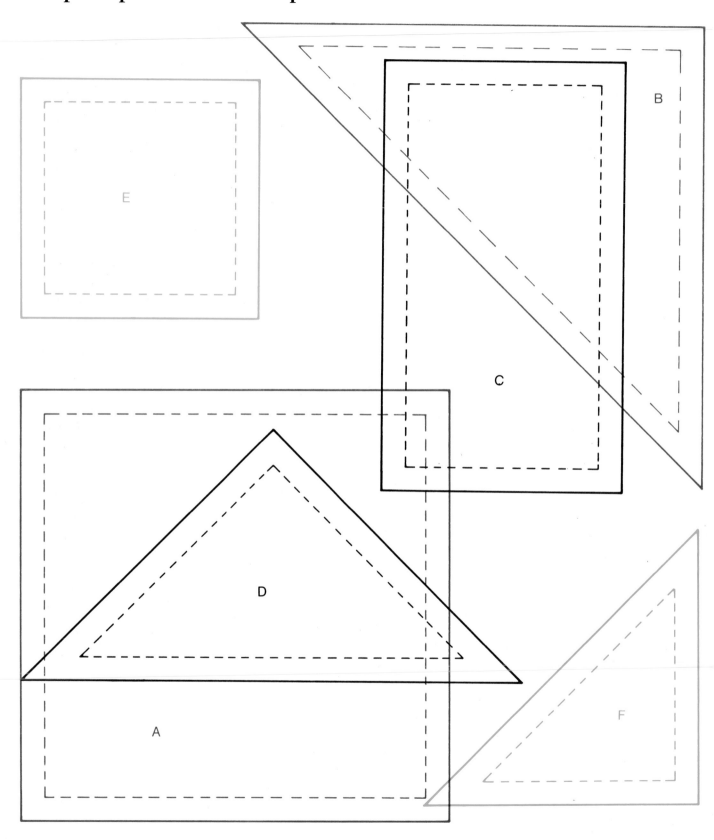

Strawberry-Garden *(1982, Brigitte Staub-Wachsmuth)*
Size 160 × 160 cm/63 × 63 in
The Nine-Patch-Variation pattern (page 26) was used for this quilt. It was made from 16 blocks, half with red as the colour of the third fabric, and half with green. The blocks were sewn directly to one another without lattice strips. The

interesting overall design was achieved by turning each successive block through ninety degrees.

The quilt gets its name from the patterned fabric which has a small strawberry design.

The four-patch block

The pattern of the four-patch block is achieved by dividing *the basic square* (12 × 12 in/30.5 × 30.5 cm) into four equal parts or patches.

Each patch can then be subdivided into triangles or squares (see diagram 2).

The rectangle marked F is not needed for the pattern blocks given in this section but is included here and with the template patterns for the sake of completeness. (Actual-size template patterns for the four-patch blocks can be found at the end of this section on page 38.)

Naturally you can use these basic elements to make up your own patterns. The easiest way to do this is to make a variety of templates in different coloured paper, cutting off the seam allowance. You can juggle these pieces around until you find a pleasing pattern. This does not apply exclusively to the four-patch block, but to all the templates except for the one-patch block.

The sewing of the four-patch block is similar to that of the nine-patch block:

First sew all the small sections together to make four large squares and then join these to form the complete block.

In the following pages, each of the four-patch patterns is given in the form of a photograph, a diagram and a short working guide.

The photo shows what the finished block looks like. The diagram alongside contains the following information:

1. Letters indicate which templates you need and how many of each.
2. The different colour tones in each diagram show the lay-out of the different fabrics. Each fabric has its own colour tone.
3. The broken lines in the diagram show the quilting lines recommended for the pattern in question.

The quilting is left until the whole quilt-top is complete, so you need not worry about these lines for the time being. Details of quilting are given on page 58.

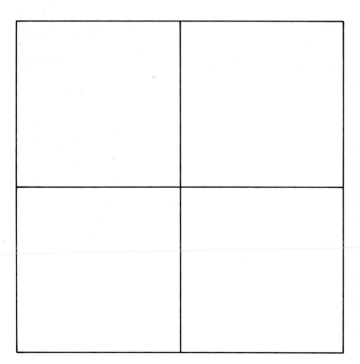

Diagram 1: *Division of the basic square into four equal patches.*

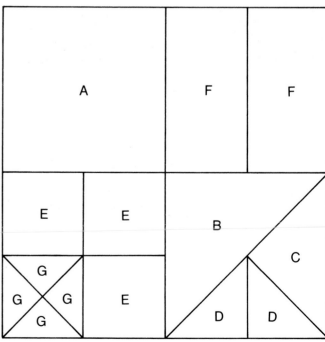

Diagram 2: *The individual patches can be further subdivided into smaller squares, rectangles and triangles.*

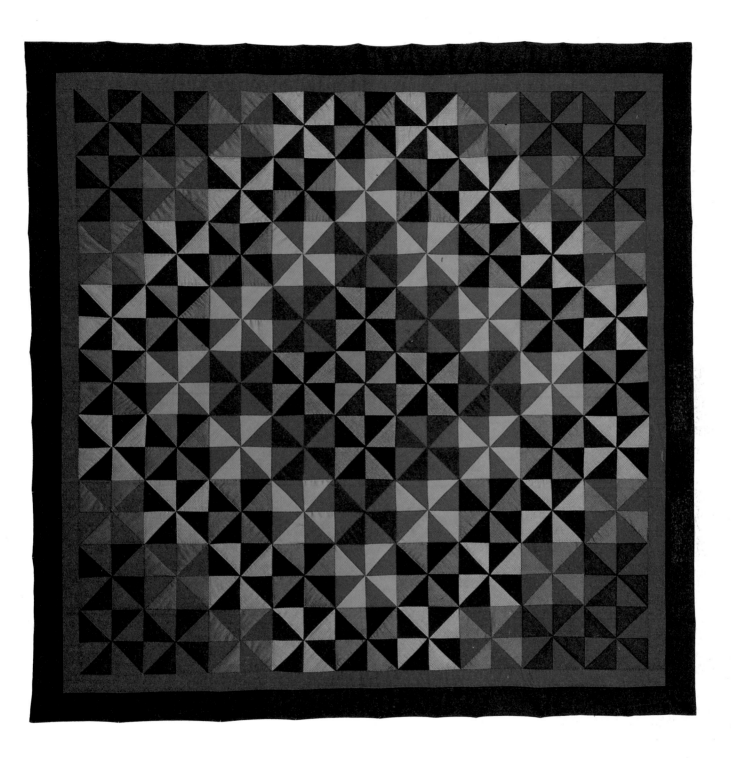

Windmill *(1983, Jutta Hormuth)*
Size: 100 × 100 cm/39¼ × 39¼ in
The basic block for this quilt is a typical four-patch pattern, the windmill. (A variation of this pattern is included on page 34 of this book.) The four patches which make up each block are simply divided into two equal triangles. Then the blocks are sewn directly together. The interesting overall design is achieved primarily by the clever use of colour and the way the individual blocks are arranged within the whole.

For materials the quiltmaker has used cotton, chintz and satin.

Traditional four-patch block patterns

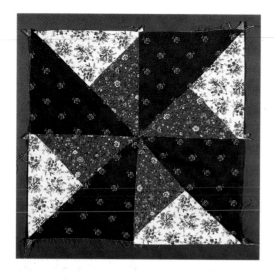

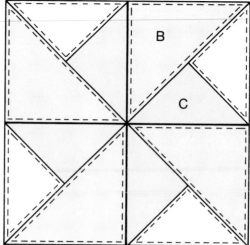

Windmill
Materials:
3 different fabrics
Templates B, C
(page 38)
Cutting:
Fabric 1: 4 of B
Fabric 2: 4 of C
Fabric 3: 4 of C

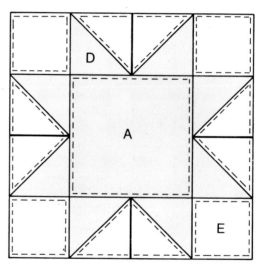

Sawtooth
Materials:
3 different fabrics
Templates A, D, E
(page 38)
Cutting:
Fabric 1: 1 of A
Fabric 2: 8 of D
Fabric 3: 8 of D
4 of E

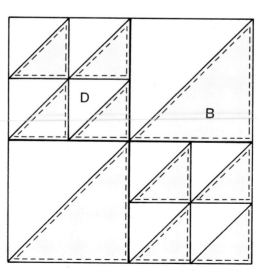

Flock of Geese
Materials:
2 different fabrics
Templates B, D
(page 38)
Cutting:
Fabric 1: 2 of B
8 of D
Fabric 2: 2 of B
8 of D

Pieced Star
Materials:
2 different fabrics
Template D (page 38)
Cutting:
Fabric 1: 16 of D
Fabric 2: 16 of D

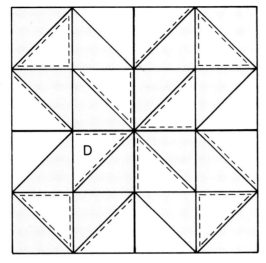

Flyfoot
Materials:
2 different fabrics
Template D (page 38)
Cutting:
Fabric 1: 16 of D
Fabric 2: 16 of D

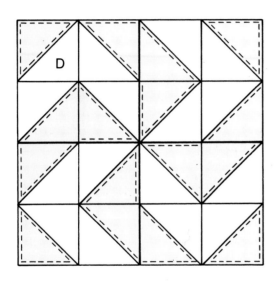

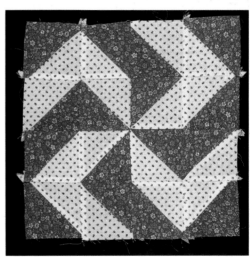

Bachelor's Puzzle
Materials:
5 different fabrics
Templates D, E
(page 38)
Cutting:
Fabric 1: 4 of D
Fabric 2: 8 of D
Fabric 3: 8 of D
Fabric 4: 4 of D
Fabric 5: 4 of E

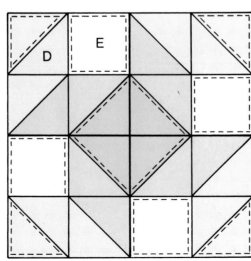

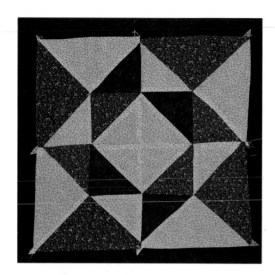

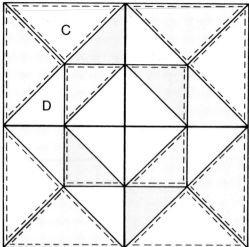

Pieced Box
Materials:
3 different fabrics
Templates C, D
(page 38)
Cutting:
Fabric 1: 4 of C
*   4 of D*
Fabric 2: 4 of C
*   8 of D*
Fabric 3: 4 of D

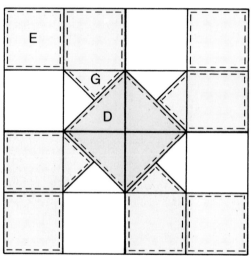

Susannah Patch
Materials:
4 different fabrics
Templates D, E, G
(page 38)
Cutting:
Fabric 1: 4 of D
Fabric 2: 4 of E
*   4 of G*
Fabric 3: 4 of E
*   4 of G*
Fabric 4: 4 of E

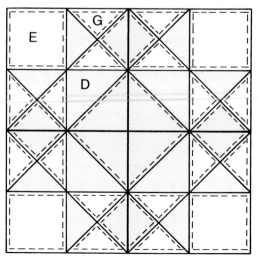

Square and Star
Materials:
3 different fabrics
Templates D, G, E
(page 38)
Cutting:
Fabric 1: 4 of D
*   8 of G*
Fabric 2: 4 of D
*   8 of G*
Fabric 3: 4 of E
*   16 of G*

Medallion-Sampler *(1983, Brigitte Staub-Wachsmuth)*
Size: 190 × 190 cm/74¾ × 74¾ in
The central block is surrounded by various friendship blocks.

The theme of the quilt, Florida, is echoed in the border of Seminole-(strip)-patchwork. (The Seminoles are an Indian tribe who still live in Florida.) The colours red, white and blue are the American national colours. A quilt like this can tell a true story. This one was made when I was living in America and was a gift from my American friends.

Template patterns for four-patch blocks

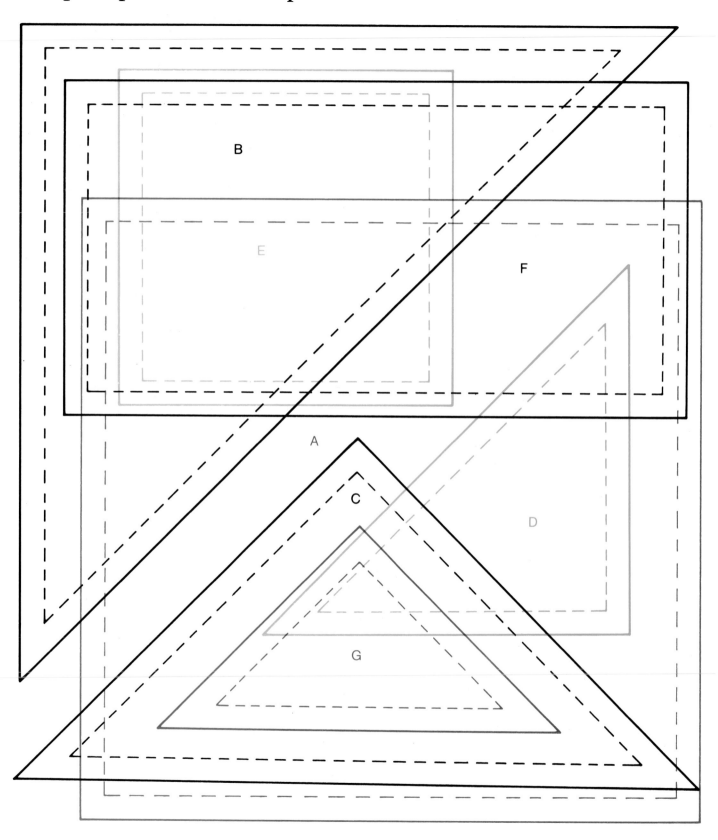

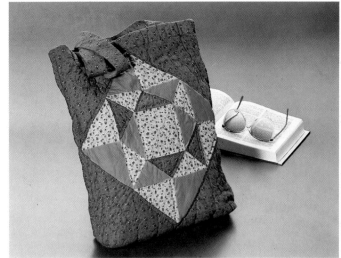

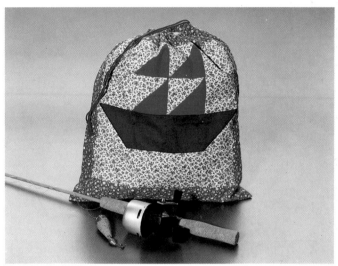

Cushion (top left)

The windmill-pattern patchwork block is first made larger with a narrow red border, 2.5 cm/1 in wide, and then a 4 cm/1½in outer border.

The patchwork part is then attached to a piece of wadding and a backing and quilted. The back of the cushion is then attached and the edges overcast on the wrong side.

Table mats (bottom left)

The patchwork block, a variation on the Sawtooth pattern, has an 8 cm/3 in strip attached to each end. The wadding and backing are added and the mats are finally quilted.

Bag (top right)

The bag is made from two patchwork blocks in the four-patch Pieced Box pattern. To make it larger a triangle is added to each corner.

The wadding and backing are then added and quilted. To finish off the bag, front and back are folded together and joined at the side seams. Don't forget to attach a handle.

Draw-string bag (bottom right)

A patchwork draw-string bag is quick to make. One block is enlarged to the required size, a piece of fabric is cut to the same size for the back of the bag and the two sewn together. Without quilting, sew up the side seams and thread a drawstring through the hemmed opening at the top. This is a good idea for a child's gym bag.

Appliquéd motifs

Templates for appliqué patterns are made in exactly the same way as the templates for the other blocks. The actual-size template patterns in this chapter, however, do *not* include a seam allowance.

The prepared templates are placed on the right side of the fabric and outlined with an impermanent marker. Then the fabric pieces are cut out allowing roughly 5 mm/⅕ in all round for seams. It is not essential for the seam allowance to be exactly the same all round, the important thing when you come to sew is that the outline should be clearly marked.

Now the edges should be turned under to the drawn line and the seam tacked with large stitches. Points, edges and corners should be turned under first and a stitch made to hold them in place before the remainder of the seam is turned. For shallow curves the seam should be lightly gathered. For sharper curves or corners you will have to snip the seam allowance several times if it is to turn under neatly. All pieces should then be ironed and laid out on a piece of cloth 31.8 cm/12½ in square (the standard patchwork block size) in accordance with the pattern. Pin each piece in place and then sew into position.

You should begin on the underside of the fabric with a knot and bring the needle up through the outside edge of the piece to be appliquéd. Then, making as small a stitch as possible, pass the needle back through the fabric backing and bring it up again 3 mm/¹⁄₁₀ in further on. This stitch (see diagram below) is used to sew around each section of appliqué until they are all firmly attached to the backing fabric. The stitches will be more or less invisible if you keep them as small as possible and use a matching thread. Finally, remove the tacks and, if you wish, finish off the block with a little embroidery. It is always a good idea to choose a plain background colour to show off the appliqué design to the best advantage.

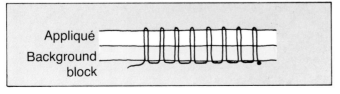

Wild Rose Appliqué Quilt (*c. 1940, property of Brigitte Staub-Wachsmuth*)
Size: 195 × 240 cm/76¾ × 94½ in
You will find full-size template patterns for this quilt on the following two pages

Template pattern for Wild Rose appliqué quilt

straight stem

rounded stem

rounded stem

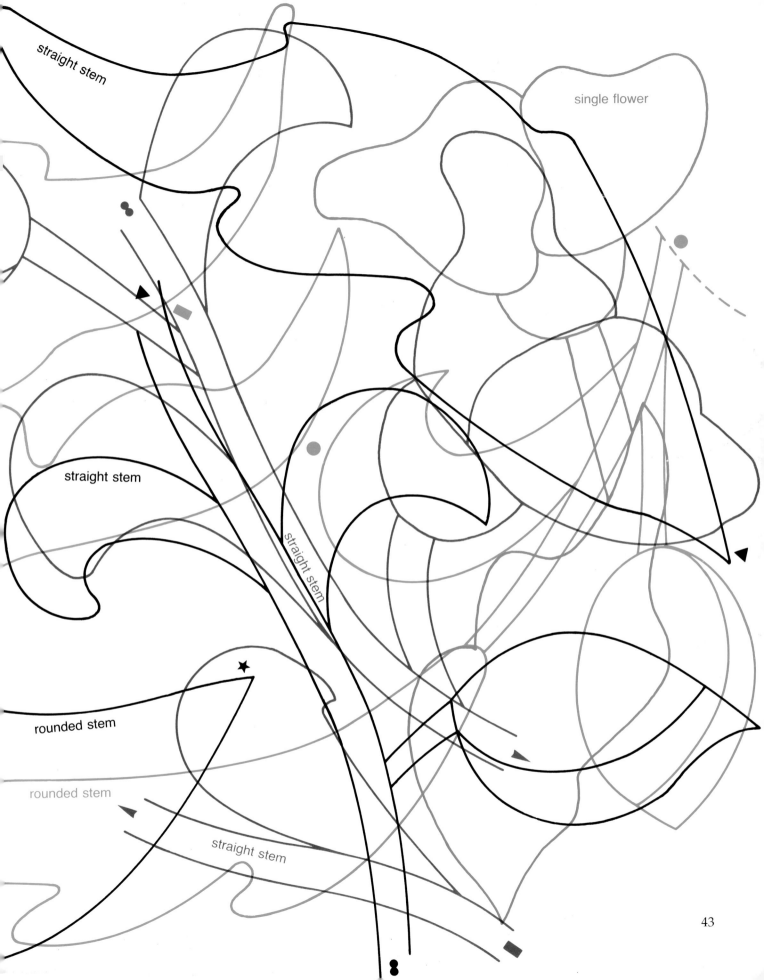

straight stem

single flower

straight stem

straight stem

rounded stem

rounded stem

straight stem

43

Shadow Sampler *(1984, Brigitte Staub-Wachsmuth)*
Size: 165 × 210 cm/65 × 82½ in
This quilt includes both patchwork and appliquéd blocks. The shadow effect is
achieved by the light and dark lattice which frames the individual blocks.

Traditional appliqué patterns

Honey Bee
Materials:
4 different fabrics
Templates A, B, C, D
(outlined in red on page 47)
Cutting:
Fabric 1: 4 of A
*   4 of B*
Fabric 2: 5 of C
Fabric 3: 4 of C
Fabric 4: 12 of D
Parts A, B and C make up the
basic block, onto which parts
D are appliquéd.

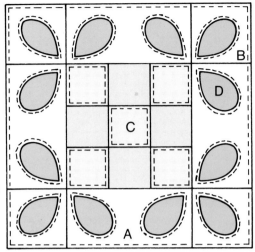

Butterfly
Materials:
3 different fabrics
Templates A, B, C
(outlined
in blue on page 47)
Cutting:
Fabric 1: 2 of A
Fabric 2: 2 of B
Fabric 3: 1 of C
None of the templates allow
for seams. The feelers are
embroidered.

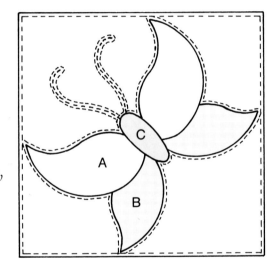

Grandmother's Fan
Materials:
4 different fabrics
Templates A, B (outlined
in black on page 47)
Cutting:
Fabric 1: 2 of B
Fabric 2: 2 of B
Fabric 3: 2 of B
Fabric 4: 1 of A
The B sections are first sewn
together and appliquéd onto a
backing. Section A is sewn on
last.

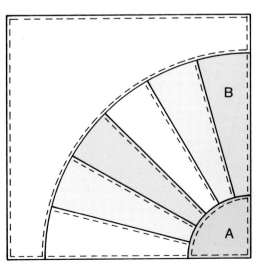

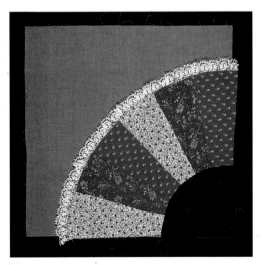

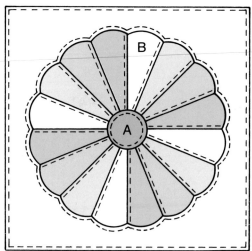

Dresden Plate
Materials:
5 different fabrics
Templates A, B (outlined
in black on this page)
Cutting:
Fabric 1: 4 of B
Fabric 2: 4 of B
Fabric 3: 4 of B
Fabric 4: 4 of B
Fabric 5: 1 of A
First sew B sections
together, then add section A.

Template patterns for appliqué designs

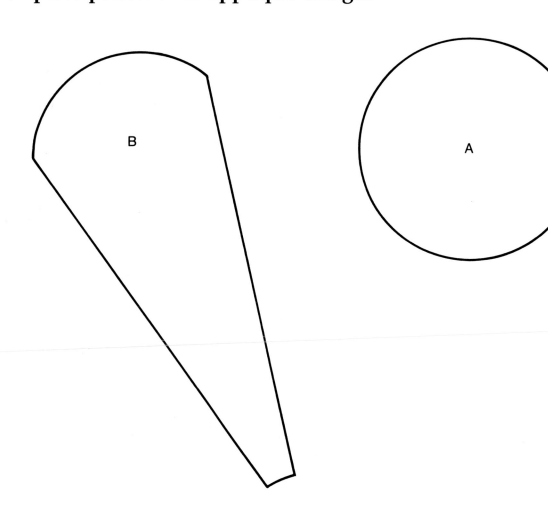

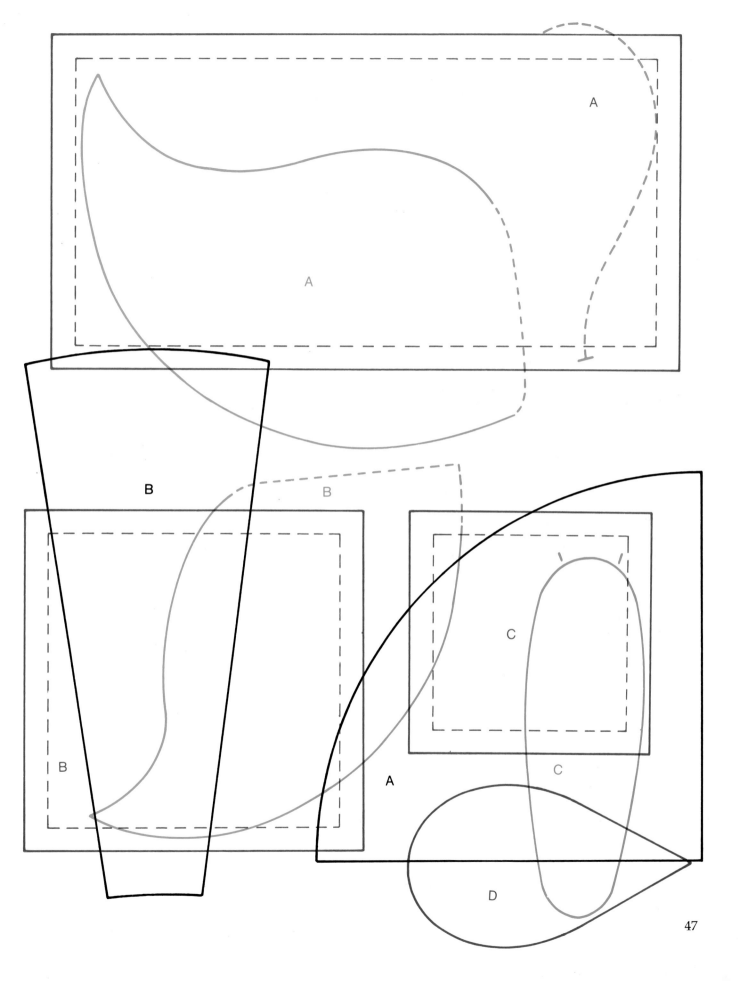

Blocks with rounded sections

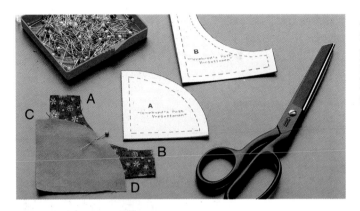

After cutting, the two sections whose rounded edges are to be joined are first folded in half to find the centre point. At this centre point pin together the two pieces of fabric, right sides together, as shown in the photo. (The letters A to D denote the corners which will be referred to in the instructions that follow.)

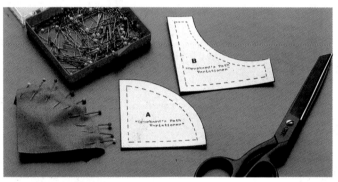

Without removing the pin that is holding the two sections together, pin corner A into position behind corner C (red fabric). Repeat for corner B, pinning it behind corner D of the red fabric. Pin the rest of the side together, using as many pins as you need to hold it firmly in position. The main thing is to use plenty of pins and to make sure that they go securely through both layers of fabric, as shown in the photo.

Now sew on whichever side the curve lies flat. In our example this is the wrong side of the red fabric. If you are machine sewing make sure that the edge of the foot follows the cut edge of the fabric exactly. If hand sewing sew along the marked seam line. Leave the pins in place until you have sewn right along the seam!

When the patch is opened out, the curved seam will lie flat and can now be ironed.

The finished round-edged patchwork sections are made up into pattern blocks in exactly the same way as the ordinary patches. First, small sections are sewn together, these are joined to make rows and finally the rows are sewn together. Rounded sections can be included in any pattern block.

The Wedding Ring design, for instance, is a one-patch block design. The two other examples, Drunkard's Path Variation and Time and Energy are four-patch patterns.

Wedding Ring Quilt *(1983, Brigitte Staub-Wachsmuth)*
Size: 140 × 140 cm/55¼ × 55¼ in
This patchwork design symbolises wedding rings and was once a popular design for wedding quilts. To make this quilt, begin by making eight complete blocks in the Wedding Ring pattern (see page 50). These patterns should be hand-sewn. First sew section B to section C. These are then joined to A. The

squares (D) are added last. These complete blocks form the corners of the quilt. To get the pattern of the interlinking rings, only the missing sections of the block have to be added each time. Patterns for the quilting lines used here can be found on page 64 outlined in red.

Traditional patterns with rounded seams

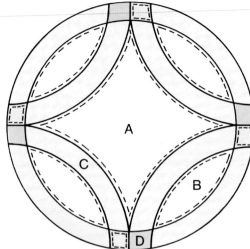

Wedding Ring
Materials:
4 different fabrics
Templates A, B, C, D
(outlined in blue on the
opposite page)
Cutting:
Fabric 1: 1 of A
4 of B
Fabric 2: 8 of C
Fabric 3: 4 of D
Fabric 4: 4 of D

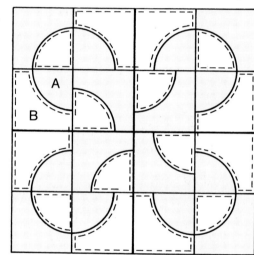

Drunkard's Path Variation
Materials:
2 different fabrics
Templates A, B (outlined
in red on the opposite
page)
Cutting:
Fabric 1: 8 of A
8 of B
Fabric 2: 8 of A
8 of B

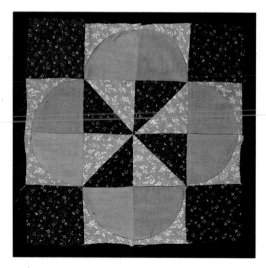

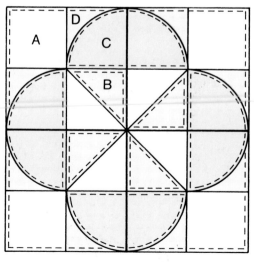

Time and Energy
Materials:
3 different fabrics
Templates A, B, C, D
(outlined in black on the
opposite page)
Cutting:
Fabric 1: 4 of A
4 of B
Fabric 2: 4 of B
8 of D
Fabric 3: 8 of C

Template patterns for blocks with rounded seams

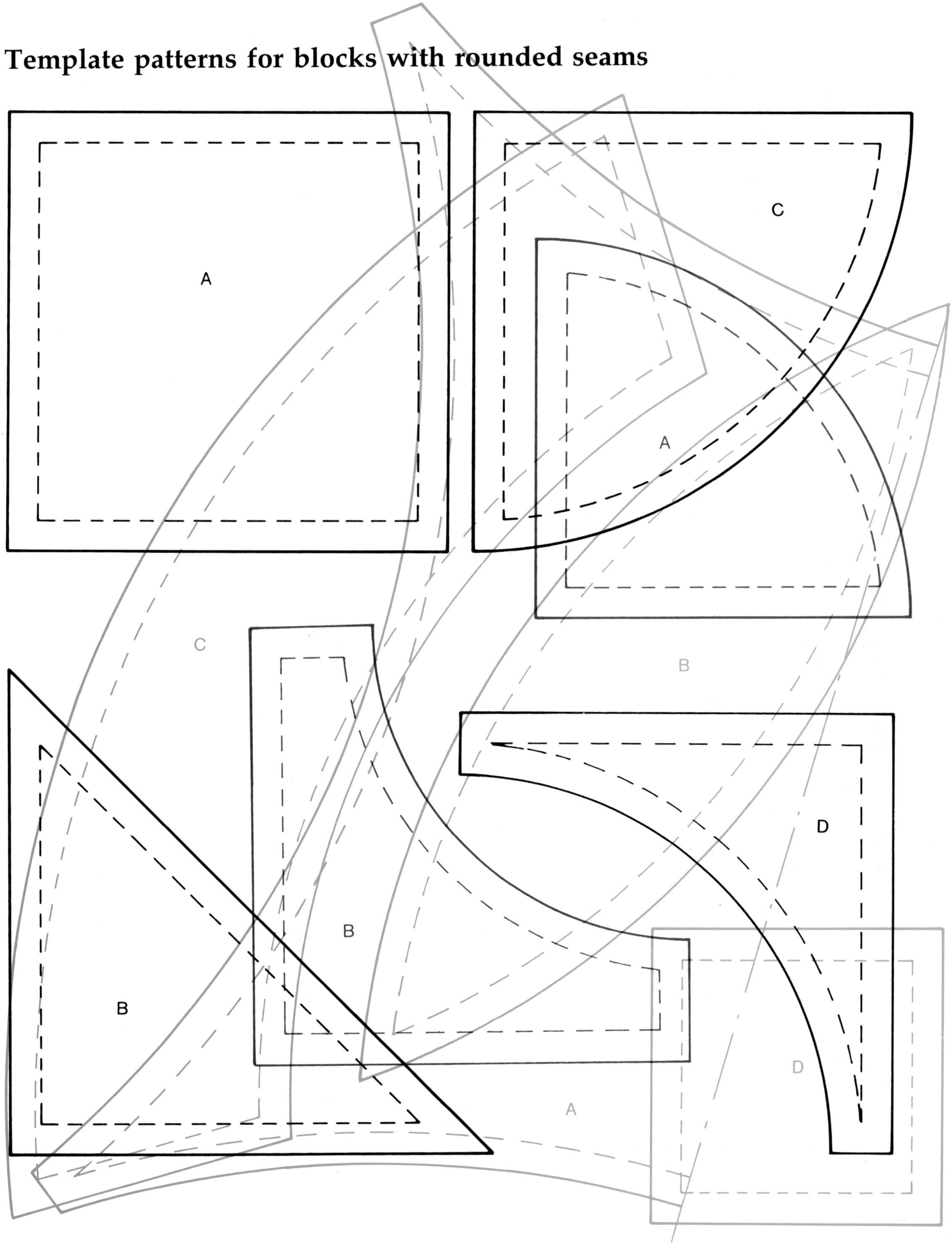

A

C

A

C

B

B

B

A

D

D

The one-patch block

A one-patch block is a quilt block which forms a whole unit rather than comprising a number of smaller squares. Templates for a one-patch block can therefore be used only for one special pattern, but by changing the colour combinations and fabric patterns the effect can be very different. Beautiful quilts have resulted from surprising combinations.

These blocks are assembled in the same way as patchwork: start by joining small sections and build up into larger units. The row-building principle should also be used here when assembling the blocks. Many of the one-patch block patterns are traditional and have a history dating back to the time of the early settlers in the United States and Canada.

Traditional one-patch blocks

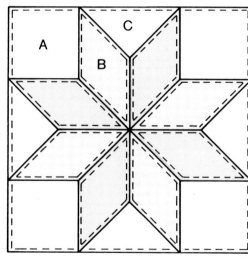

Lonely Star
Materials:
3 different fabrics
Templates A, B, C (outlined in red on page 55)
Cutting:
Fabric 1: 4 of B
Fabric 2: 4 of B
Fabric 3: 4 of A
*   4 of C*
This pattern is best sewn by hand. Sew the B sections together and then insert sections A and C.

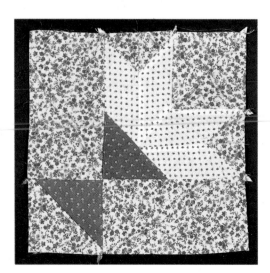

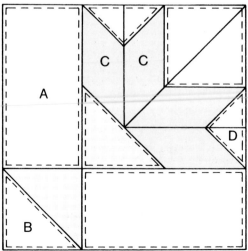

Basket of Scraps
Materials:
3 different fabrics
Templates A, B, C, D (outlined in black on page 55)
Cutting:
Fabric 1: 2 of A
*   3 of B*
*   4 of D*
Fabric 2: 2 of B
Fabric 3: 2 of C, 2 of C′ C′:
*   Use template C reversed.*

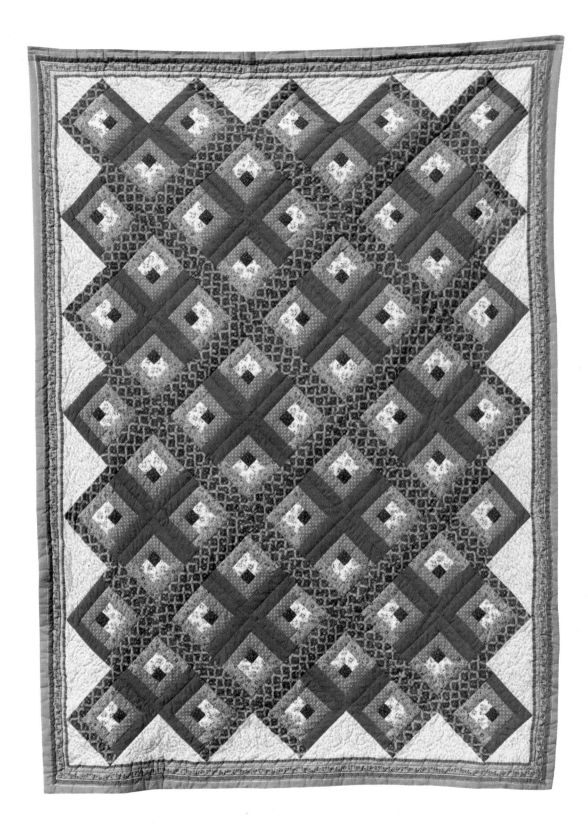

Log Cabin Fence *(1983, Brigitte Staub-Wachsmuth)*
Size: 175 × 235 cm/69 × 92½ in
A modern version of the popular traditional Log Cabin pattern

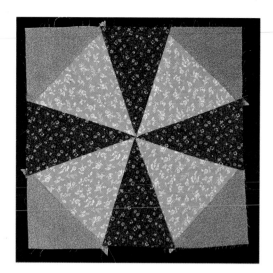

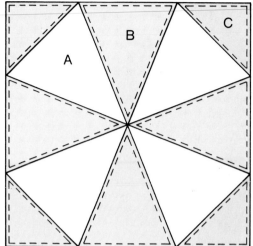

Kaleidoscope

Materials:
3 different fabrics
Templates A, B, C (outlined in blue on the opposite page)
Cutting:
Fabric 1: 4 of A
Fabric 2: 4 of B
Fabric 3: 4 of C

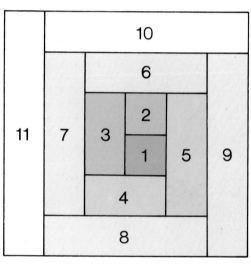

Log Cabin

Materials:
6 different fabrics, ranging from light to dark
Templates A, B (outlined in green on the opposite page)
Cutting:
Cut the fabric into strips using template B and sew together in the order shown by the numbers in the diagram. Four of these squares together make the Log Cabin pattern.

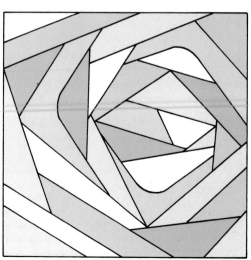

Crazy Quilt

Materials:
Scraps of fabric of any shape, size or design.
Please note:
Individual scraps can be sewn together in any way you like. All rounded-seams are overcast. In a traditional crazy quilt the layers are held together simply by embroidery and are not quilted.

Template patterns for one-patch blocks

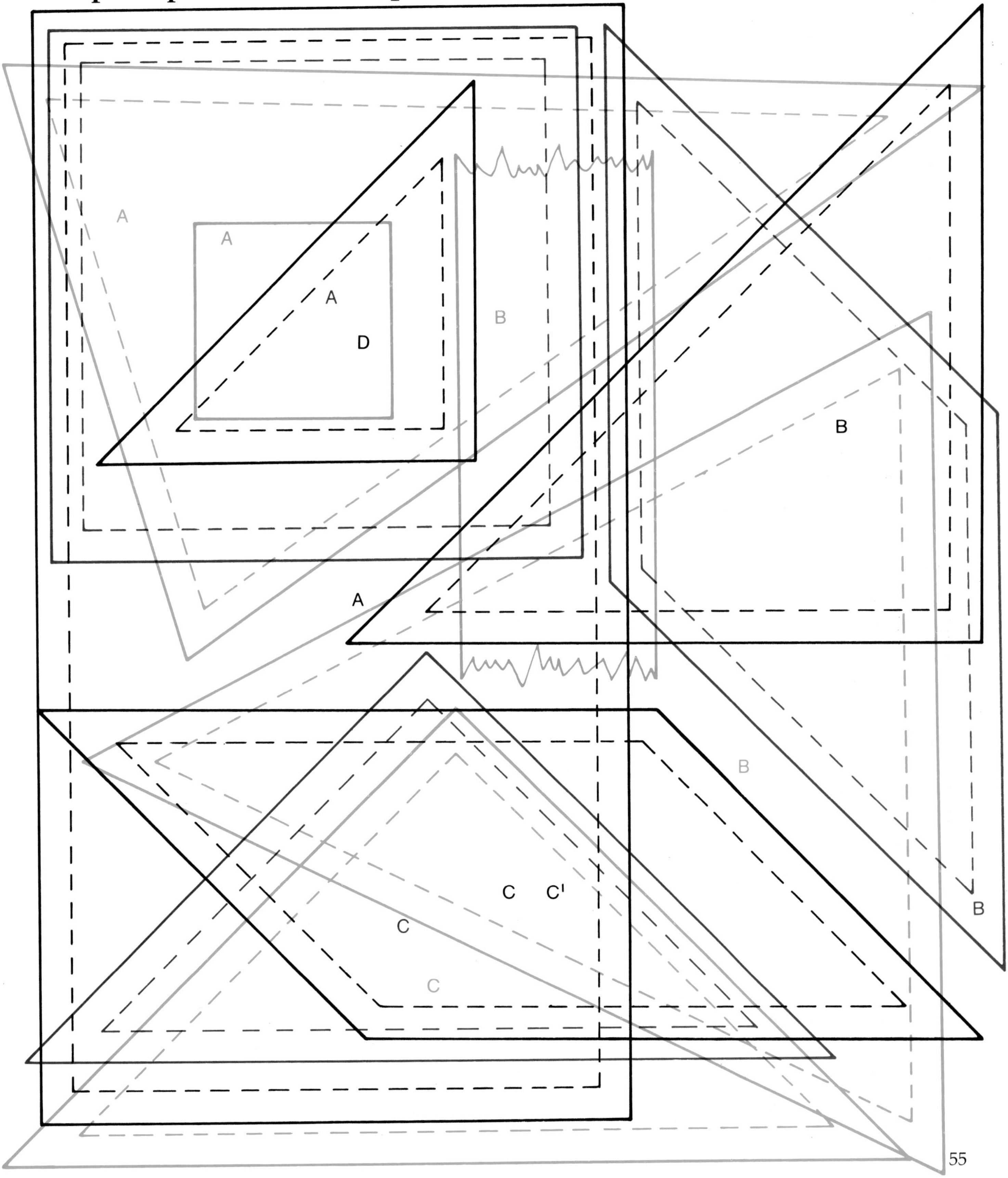

A

A

A

D

B

B

A

B

C C'

C

C

B

Getting ready for quilting

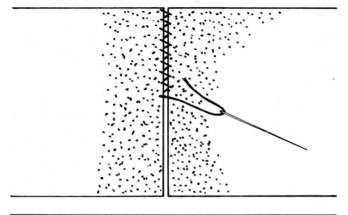

Wadding

The wadding, which goes between the quilt top and quilt backing, should be the same size as the patchwork quilt-top. Unfortunately it is sold only in 90 and 140 cm/ $35\frac{1}{2}$ and $55\frac{1}{4}$ in widths. For any other width, lengths will have to be cut and sewn together along the long edge. Sew the two pieces together using rough zig-zag stitches, making sure that the two pieces butt up to each other rather than overlapping.

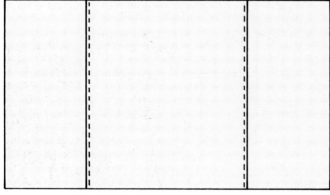

The backing

Cut the backing fabric generously because it will be used for the side seams of the quilt. It should be cut at least 10 cm/4 in larger than the quilt-top all round. The backing should be washed and the selvage edges cut off before making up. If you need two widths of material for the backing, the first width should be halved length-ways. The two halves are then sewn to the long sides of the second width. These seams should be ironed flat to one side.

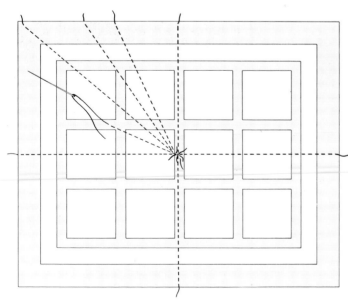

Tacking

When each layer of the quilt is ready, the three layers have to be tacked together to hold them firmly in place during the next stage of the operation, the quilting. First spread the backing on a large table or on the floor and smooth it out. Then place the wadding on it. Next, carefully lay the quilt-top on top. Make sure that all three layers meet exactly at the corners. The tacking stitches should radiate out from the centre. Do not secure either the beginning or the end of the threads with knots or backstitches. The ends of the threads should be left to hang loose. The tacking needs to be able to give when you come to the quilting otherwise it will tension the fabric and make the quilt-top uneven. Put in enough lines of tacking so as to leave no more than a hand's width between them at the edges of the quilt (see diagram).

Finishing off the quilt

Closing the quilt

You should not finish off the edges of the quilt until all other work on it is complete. The wadding can stretch during quilting and if you have already sewn the edges they will have to be unpicked.

The wadding is trimmed to the size of the quilt top. The backing is cut 10 cm/4 in larger all round than the wadding and quilt top. This allows enough fabric to be folded double over the edge of the quilt top. It is used double because it is always the edges of a quilt that wear first.

At the corners, the two edges are simply folded one over the other and pinned. Only when you have pinned the whole border should you begin hemming. Make sure that the border is of equal width all round, for when the quilt is finished this hem serves as an extra border and it would not look very attractive if its width was not uniform.

To hem the quilt, try to use invisible hemming stitches. The stitches will be easiest to conceal if you use a thread the same colour as the backing or the quilt top. If the border is wide it is a good idea to quilt it to prevent the wadding slipping.

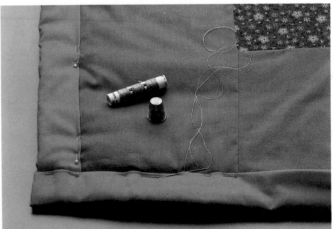

Hanging attachment

If the finished quilt is to be used as a wall-hanging, it will need a hanging attachment. To avoid straining and eventually tearing any of the quilt seams, you should use a method which distributes the weight evenly. The best way is to fix the quilt to the wall on a wooden slat. To do this take a piece of the backing fabric and make a pocket, as shown in the diagram. Make sure that the pocket is wide enough for the wooden slat to slide in easily. Fasten the pocket to the back of the quilt using rough hemming stitches (if you make them large they are easy to take out if you want to at some later stage), push in the wooden slat and support with two or three nails.

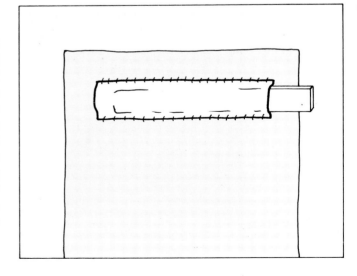

Quilting

As well as holding the three layers of the quilt in place, quilting also serves to decorate the quilt in a style in keeping with the rest of the quilt top and to give solidity to the patchwork patterns. In some quilts, the quilting lines are the most prominent part of the design. In others they form a subtle, very pleasing, textured effect.

The author working at her quilting frame. This frame tensions the piece of work ready for quilting

The quilting template

First look for a suitable design on pages 62ff and copy it onto tracing paper. Stick the tracing onto an ordinary sheet of paper and reinforce the template by covering the two sides with transparent cling-film. Now take a paper knife and cut slits at intervals along the quilting lines. Make sure you leave enough behind to prevent the whole design falling apart.

Marking the quilting lines

The quilting template is purposely made from soft, pliable paper rather than cardboard, so that it will lie better on the pliable fabric. Place the template on the quilt and mark the quilting lines with an impermanent mark.

For a running border – like the black pattern on page 63 – you will have to use the template repeatedly until you have a long enough border. The choice of quilting designs is entirely a matter of personal preference.

Starting and finishing the thread

For quilting it is best to use a strong cotton-covered polyester thread or a special quilting thread. The thread you choose should be fine enough to be easy to work with, but strong enough not to break. For quilting you need a short, sharp needle. Ask in a handicraft shop for special quilting needles (a no. 7 is a useful size). These are stronger than ordinary sewing needles and do not bend. The smaller the needle, the finer the stitches you can make with it.

To begin quilting make a four-layer knot in your thread. Push the needle into the quilt from the top and pull the knot into the middle layer (wadding) of the quilt, by pulling the thread with your left hand while lifting the fabric slightly with the needle in your right hand, so that the knot can slip through the fabric. There is no problem with this if you are sewing on cotton.

When you come to the end of the thread, repeat the process. Make a knot in the thread just above the fabric and pull it as described above through the quilt top into the wadding.

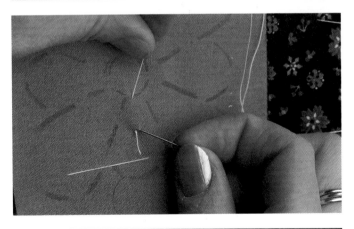

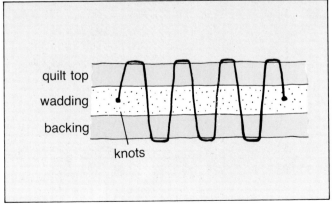

The quilting stitch

In quilting, a running stitch is used. The stitching holds the three layers of material together but it should also allow for a certain amount of movement between the layers. A running stitch serves both these purposes whereas backstitch would not. (The diagram on page 59 shows how the thread passes through the three layers.)

The stitching should be as small and even as possible. Quilting is done with the right or left hand pushing the needle into the quilt top (see photo). The other hand should be under the quilt to return the needle to the top.

The quilting lines

When quilting, one should always work outwards from the centre of the quilt. This is very important because it is the only way to prevent the quilt puckering. You should also work outwards from the centre of each pattern block – in our example you would start with the flower at the centre of the Box Quilt pattern. Do not leave an area larger than $10\,cm^2/4\,in^2$ between quilting lines. Remember: all the quilting should be completed before you finish off the edges of the quilt (for instructions on how to do this see page 57).

In principle it is purely a matter of personal taste and imagination which patterns you use when quilting. But the traditional patterns included in previous chapters have set quilting lines which should be used with them. In the diagrams found alongside the photos of the completed patch, these quilting lines are marked with a broken line. Refer to these diagrams to find out how you should quilt the individual pattern-blocks in your sampler quilt. Always remember to start at the centre of the block.

The quilting frame

You will find quilting much easier if you can tension the quilt in a quilting frame. All quilting frames are large enough to allow for a complete pattern block to be tensioned at any one time. When attached to the frame the three layers of fabric are held firm and cannot slide during quilting, which avoids ugly puckering. It also leaves you both hands free to work with. The right hand pushes the needle into the quilt from the top side while the left hand remains under the quilt to return the needle to the top in the right place for the next stitch. (If you are left-handed the opposite will, of course, apply.)

Breadfruit Quilt *(1983, Brigitte Staub-Wachsmuth)*
Size 60 × 60 cm/23½ × 23½ in
This motif comes from Hawaii, which is why these quilts are often referred to as Hawaiian Quilts. The appliqué motif in the centre was cut initially from paper folded into four, and sewn on by hand. A distinctive feature of the Hawaiian Quilts are the close-set quilting lines which run in waves around the central design. Native Hawaiians believe that a Hawaiian Quilt must always bear the breadfruit motif. It a quiltmaker can successfully reproduce the design, this quilt will bring her luck and success in every future venture.

61

Quilting patterns

Quilting pattern for a pair of 10 cm/4 in border
(eg. 'Swallows of Capistrano', page 67)

Quilting pattern for a
6 cm/2⅓ in border

Various flower patterns

Flower pattern page 69

Quilting pattern
for a centrepiece

Flower pattern
(eg 'Lonely Star', page 69)

Quilting pattern with corner for a 10 cm/4 in border
(eg 'La Grande Dahlia', page 66)

Feather pattern

Quilting pattern for a centrepiece
(eg. 'Wedding Ring', page 49)

Quilting Pattern for a
6—8 cm/2⅓—3¼ in wide Border
(eg. 'Stain Glass Quilt', page 73)

64

Quilting pattern
for corner triangle

Quilting pattern for
16–20 cm/6⅓—7¾ in
square

Quilting pattern for a
15 cm/6 in wide border

65

Quilt Gallery

The quilts and patchwork items illustrated on this and the following pages show the wide variety of quilt designs that are possible. Even simple patterns can be highly effective if a little thought goes into lay-out and choice of colours.

I hope these examples will inspire you to experiment with techniques and patterns and to go beyond the familiar classic designs. The appeal of quilting will become apparent as you begin to design your own quilts, bringing order and beauty to everyday objects.

La Grande Dahlia Quilt (*opposite page*)
1984, Brigitte Staub-Wachsmuth
Size: 190 × 190 cm/74¾ × 74¾ in
This design is made from 16 crescent-shaped strips which, when sewn together, produce larger and larger diamond shapes. (The points of the crescents are at the centre, the more rounded ends towards the outside.) The star at the centre and the outer yellow pieces were added later and the completed dahlia sewn onto a toning background.

This design is found not only in patchwork but also as inlay work in old furniture.

Swallows of Capistrano Medallion Quilt (*below*)
1984, Brigitte Staub-Wachsmuth
Size: 175 × 175 cm/69 × 69 in
A medallion quilt is one in which a central motif is surrounded by various, ever-widening borders until the quilt is the desired size. The central motif of this quilt is made from eight identical cone-shaped pieces, which are themselves made up from smaller triangles.

The contrast between light and dark in the outer border creates a three-dimensional effect.

Untitled Quilt (opposite page)
1984, Adelheid Gubsek
Size: 180 × 240 cm/70¾ × 94½ in
This quilt consists of 1750, 4 cm/1½ in squares. All the squares were arranged according to shade and then sewn first into rows 240 cm/94½ in in length. In joining the rows to form the quilt top the symmetrical arrangement of the squares was offset by moving some rows out of place and turning others upside down. The result is a quilt that has all the qualities of a work of modern art.

Lonely Star Quilt (*below*)
1985. Brigitte Staub-Wachsmuth
Size: 170 × 170 cm/67 × 67 in
The Lonely Star is one of the most popular traditional patchwork patterns. (Instructions for making this pattern can be found on page 52.) The basic star has been enlarged and points added to the outside with concentric rings of matching diamond-shaped pieces. Four squares form the corners and four triangles complete the central square. The patchwork border echoes the colours used for the central square.

Untitled Quilt (below)
1983, Katherine Picot
Size: 160 × 160 cm/63 × 63 in
*This quilt is made using two four-patch blocks; one is the
Sawtooth pattern and the other a variation on the four-patch
pattern (see page 32). By variously changing the arrangement
of these two pattern blocks an interesting design has been
achieved and the effect is emphasised by the use of colour. A
combination of silk and cotton has gone into the making of this
quilt.*

Storm at Sea (opposite page)
Helle Eggebrecht, 1980
Size: 173 × 205 cm/68 × 80¾ in
*Storm at Sea is a traditional American patchwork pattern,
intended to remind people of the long voyage to the New
World.*

*The 'waves' which run diagonally across the quilt are an
optical illusion. All the seams in the pattern are straight, as
you can see if you look closely.*

Flowers in Window Quilt (*opposite*)
1984, Brigitte Staub-Wachsmuth
Size: 135 × 175 cm/53¼ × 69 in
An extremely modern approach to quilting. Inspired by the work of the Dutch painter Piet Mondrian, the pattern of rectangles has a transparent feel to it. The flowers and the vase were appliquéd onto the quilt at the second stage. The contrast between the cold background colours and the warm tones of the flowers is emphasised by the contrast between straight lines and curves in the overall design.

Stained Glass Window Quilt (*below*)
1984, Brigitte Staub-Wachsmuth
Size: 105 × 115 cm/41¼ × 45¼ in
This modern quilt was inspired by the Tiffany lamps and windows. All the decorative elements were appliquéd to the quilt top with the help of a dark blue bias strip. This gives the impression of a leaded window. The flowers have also been given the extra padding of the Trapunto technique to make them stand out more. The close-set quilting lines effectively emphasise the shapes in the design.

Crossing Winds Quilt (opposite)
1985, Brigitte Staub-Wachsmuth
Size: 175 × 245 cm/69× 96½in
The whole quilt is made from Log Cabin blocks (see one-patch block, page 54).

The arrangement both of the individual strips within the blocks and of the blocks themselves is unusual. The block effect of the individual patches is lost amidst a new overall design. Since the quilting lines are intended to emphasise the pattern of the individual block, they have been made as discreet as possible.

Points of the Compass Quilt (below)
1984, Schnuppe von Gwinner
Size: 240 × 240 cm/94½ × 94½in
In this patchwork quilt, traditional principles of patchwork have been used in an unfamiliar way. Although it is made from blocks, it has the feel of a Medallion Quilt. A variety of materials have gone into its making and it is left up to the onlooker to decide which colours or which shapes are dominant.

Block Combinations

1983, Anna Zimmermann

Size: 100 × 100 cm/39¾ × 39¾ in

Two different blocks have been combined to make this wall quilt. The colour gradations within the blocks create a three-dimensional effect. An interesting feature of the work is the quilting lines which purposely underline and emphasise the geometric forms of the blocks. Quilt designs are becoming more unusual, but are still highly treasured.

76

Star in a Circle *(right)*
1983, Brigitte Staub-Wachsmuth
Size: 155 × 155 cm/61 × 61 in
This round quilt is intended for use as a
table-cloth. The star at the centre is six
Log Cabin blocks arranged to form a six-
pointed star.

Summer Quilt
(below and bottom right)
1984, Brigitte Staub-Wachsmuth
Size: 110 × 110 cm/43¼ × 43¼ in
This table-cloth is reversible. Each side is
different in colour but uses the same Log
Cabin pattern. The two sides are sewn
together with no wadding between,
hence the name Summer Quilt. This type
of bedcover is especially popular in the
southern USA.

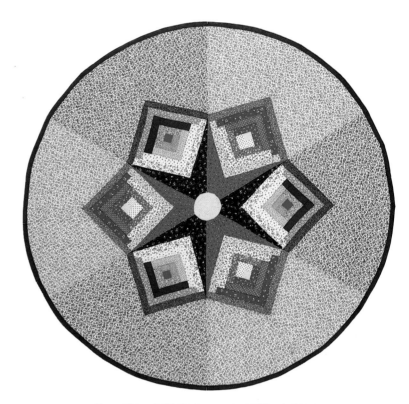

77

Georg's Quilt (*opposite*)
1984, Brigitte Staub-Wachsmuth
Size: 170 × 220 cm/67 × 86½ in
This quilt immortalises 12 of my son Georg's earliest drawings. The pictures were traced from the originals onto a light-coloured fabric and then coloured with permanent fabric paints to match the originals. Like the originals, all the drawings are of different sizes.

Patrick's Quilt (*above and top right*)
1982, Brigitte Staub-Wachsmuth
Size 165 × 200 cm/65 × 78¾ in
The top and reverse of Patrick's Quilt. The quilt was made along the same lines as Georg's Quilt. In keeping with the childish drawings, a border of elephants has been used for the quilting.

Children's waistcoats (*right*)
1984, Brigitte Staub-Wachsmuth
Patchwork and quilting can also be used to make clothes. Both of these quilted waistcoats are decorated with an appliquéd cowboy motif designed by the children themselves. Items of clothing like these need to be quilted extremely carefully to prevent the warming wadding moving with wear.

Acknowledgements
Front cover photograph: Fotostudio Burock, Wiesbaden/
Naurod, Ilia Starkovsky, Würenlos, Switzerland
The publishers thank the following for supplying
photographs of their work: Helle Eggebrecht, Felisa Erb-
Mena, Adekheid Gubsek, Jutta Hormuth, Katharine Picot,
Schnuppe von Gwinner, Brigitte Staub-Wachsmuth and
Anna Zimmerman. They also thank Pfaff for permission to
photograph the Pfaff Creative sewing machine.
Front cover quilt: Swallows of Capistrano, Brigitte Staub-
Wachsmuth
Quilt on page 1: Lonely Star, Brigitte Staub-Wachsmuth
Pages 2–3: Patchwork blocks, Brigitte Staub-Wachsmuth
Line drawings: Rolf Dähler, Bad Schwalbach

First published 1988 by
The Hamlyn Publishing Group,
Michelin House,
81 Fulham Road,
London SW3 6RB

First impression 1988

ISBN 0 600 55862 2

Printed by Mandarin Offset, Hong Kong